Free to Learn

FIVE IDEAS FOR A JOYFUL UNSCHOOLING LIFE

PAM LARICCHIA

Published by
Living Joyfully Enterprises
Erin, Ontario

ISBN: 978-0-9877333-2-0

Edited by Alexandra Peace.

Cover photography and design by Lissy Laricchia,
lissyelle.com.

DEDICATION

I have been learning from my kids, Joseph, Lissy, and Michael, since they were born. We have been living together joyfully through laughter and tears, consternation and celebration, Harry Potter and Zelda. Each day is new and exciting, even if we stay in our pyjamas, and our conversations are always interesting and thought-provoking! They are shining examples to me of staying true to yourself, especially through the challenging times, and for that I dedicate this book to them.

LOVE YOU!

CONTENTS

What you'll find in *Free to Learn*

Acknowledgments   xi

INTRODUCTION   1

Hi, I'm Pam Laricchia, nice to meet you.

What Is Unschooling?   4
    Welcome to the wonderful world of
unschooling.

Learning About Learning   7
    This book will discuss the ideas behind
unschooling and extend them into day-to-
day living. Don't just skim through the
ideas, as logical as they may seem. Really
live with them. Let your mind ruminate on
them as you go about your day.

IDEA ONE: REAL LEARNING   11

Paradigm Shift: Instead of looking at learning
from a teacher's point of view, look at it from
the learner's point of view. Real learning is best
defined by the learner precisely because it can
only take place *in* the learner, regardless of any
teaching being done *around* him or her.

At first it may seem like a small shift of focus, looking through the learner's eyes instead of the teacher's—almost semantics—but this shift is the key to observing real learning. How do we get there?

Learning versus Teaching   12

What Is Learning?   16

Building a View of the World   20

Deschooling   23

IDEA TWO: FOLLOWING THEIR INTERESTS   29

Paradigm Shift: Learning need not be defined as exclusively occurring in classrooms, during school hours, with those of school age. It can be found everywhere, at anytime, and can happen at any age.

People—and children are people—enjoy learning things that are useful to them now, and they learn best when they are interested and engaged.

Where Is Learning Found?   30

Connections Create the Web of Learning   38

Embracing Passions   42

IDEA THREE: CHOICES   50

Paradigm Shift: Instead of learning *what* choices to make, it's better to learn *how* to make informed choices.

Unschooling children are picking up skills and gathering information all the time, but at the same time they are learning how to navigate the world. How to make choices and decisions in both unique and everyday situations is a key life skill. How do we help them gain experience with this?

Judging Choices   51

Learning From Living   55

Quitting Activities   61

IDEA FOUR: INSTEAD OF NO   67

Paradigm Shift: Saying *no* can make life seem easier in the moment but saying *yes* encourages children to explore their world and cultivates their ability to live confidently in it.

The reflex, almost automatic, *no* accomplishes so much: it reminds the child where the power in the relationship sits; it discourages messes and hassles; and eventually it deters the child from bothering the parent in the first place. But what if those aren't your goals?

Analyzing Situations   68

Rules versus Principles   70

Moving to Principles   73

IDEA FIVE: LIVING TOGETHER   77

Paradigm Shift: It can seem that parents have, by virtue of age and childbirth, earned a position of power, but everyone in the family has important needs and wants and can have a voice.

Children are often the second-class citizens of the mainstream family. Does giving them a voice in the family lead to chaos?

Learning to Live with Others   78

Learning about Themselves   82

Moving on Out   93

PUTTING IT ALL TOGETHER 97

References 102

Additional Reading 104

ACKNOWLEDGMENTS

First, I want to thank my lovely editor, Alex Peace, for an awesome job. I always looked forward to our conversations, excitedly opening her emails to read her insightful comments and share virtual laughs around the minutiae of grammar. That said, any errors that still reside in the manuscript are my responsibility alone.

When I first came across unschooling and started researching, I was thrilled to find people online willing to share their thoughts and experiences. There are a few people specifically that I am so thankful were around: Anne Ohman, Sandra Dodd (SandraDodd.com), Kelly Lovejoy, and Joyce Fetteroll (JoyfullyRejoycing.com). They were instrumental sources of information and inspiration on my unschooling journey.

I'd like to thank Sandra Dodd and Cindy Bablitz for reading an early draft of the manuscript. I value the time they took to share their helpful comments and encouragement.

I'm also deeply thankful for Anne Ohman and the wonderful friendship we've developed over the years. She is a strong unschooling advocate and her support has been invaluable, as has her willingness to read my email ramblings over the years as I teased out my own learning connections.

Finally, I am very grateful to Rocco Laricchia for his willingness to question the mainstream education system alongside me and find the answers that worked best for our family.

INTRODUCTION

Hi, I'm Pam Laricchia. Our family is a wonderful web of three teenage children (Joseph, Lissy, and Michael), me, and my husband, Rocco. We've been happily unschooling in Ontario, Canada since 2002. Nice to meet you.

As background, I thought I'd share a bit about my life before, and my journey to, unschooling. Having earned an Engineering and Management degree through a unique five-year university program, I was firmly entrenched in the public and post-secondary education system, as were all my family and friends. Soon after, I was happily married and had children. But even as my parenting began veering from the mainstream, it didn't occur to me to question the system when my eldest reached school age. I do remember thinking it would be an interesting ride when we walked out of Joseph's junior kindergarten teacher interview, during which he didn't say a word to answer her questions. He smiled and explained to me that he didn't feel like talking to her today, but that he'd speak to her once he started school. I laughed and tousled his hair.

In those first years some teachers were more flexible, while others were quite determined to shave off his uniqueness. I researched, I left my career to stay home full-time, and I worked with his teachers and principals to try to help them better understand him. I even gave a presentation about spirited kids at a teacher's meeting and donated books to the library for other parents. Most of the teachers understood what I was talking about, but their feedback was that they don't have the time to work with kids outside the personalities and learning styles that mesh with the classroom setting. The kids have to fit the surroundings, not the other way around. It became clear to me that he would not thrive in public school. In my continued quest to find a learning environment that worked well for him, I found a specialized private school. The environment was better—the teachers and staff are being paid to work outside the typical lines—but still not great.

Then, through still more research, I came across the concept of homeschooling and was thrilled to discover it was legal where we lived. Rocco and I discussed it at length over the next couple of weeks and realized that there seemed no downside to trying it out for a year; if it didn't work out they could return to school. It was March Break and none of the kids went back. They were ecstatic with their newly-found playtime and I was now happily researching homeschooling. I soon discovered the notion of unschooling and after a couple weeks of trying to entice them to do some workbooks, I realized I was hindering, not helping, their learning. We spent the next months deschooling and living and having a great time. We still are!

There were five ideas along the way that really helped me to shift my mindset and to understand the potential of unschooling. Of course I didn't know that these would turn out to be such influential ideas for me. At the time I was just deeply immersed in learning all I could about unschooling and living joyfully with my children.

And I loved learning about unschooling! I still do. As I began to more fully understand the common issues surrounding unschooling, I was inspired to help others learn about it as well. I began by developing a website, and named it livingjoyfully.ca because even at that point I understood that that is what it all boils down to for me—that living joyfully, living *fully* with joy, leads to an immense amount of real learning. For both myself and for my kids.

Eventually my joy in helping others learn about unschooling (along with inspiration from Kelly Lovejoy's Live and Learn conferences based in the US) led me to host an annual unschooling conference in the Toronto area. With six years of the conference under my belt, my goal remained firm: to bring unschooling families together face to face in a relaxed and supportive environment that is conducive to learning more about unschooling, not only from the speakers but also from each other.

I've had the idea for this book in my head for a few years, but I wasn't comfortable taking the next step. I wanted to share my learning journey, but I didn't feel like I was experienced enough to speak with conviction; I didn't feel it in my bones. Every year or so when I read over the outline, I liked it more and more. But when I took a look at it again in the fall of 2009, I felt absolutely and wonderfully overwhelmed with all that I had to say about these ideas. It was finally time to write and I dove in.

So here's what I've learned.

What Is Unschooling?

When I first became a parent I was woefully unaware of my options when it came to my children's education. School is mandatory, right? That's why there are attendance laws and truant officers. I didn't know anybody who had questioned that. Public schooling was the one and only way for children to learn, (except for private school, but that was an expensive and out-of-reach option). The kids went to public school and I worked hard to make the best of it for them.

Then I came across the concept of homeschooling-kids learning outside of school (usually based out of their home, though sometimes out of the family's RV or boat). I was thrilled to discover that the school system was not the only legal option available in Canada (or in many other countries). We had a choice! This was a profound realization for me, and has been for many parents. You have a choice.

As parents, whether you choose public, private, or alternative school, homeschooling or unschooling, the act of making a conscious, well-informed choice regarding your child's learning environment is a crucial step. It is part of your journey as their supportive partner in life.

And remember, any choice you make now is not cast in stone. You can change your mind as your experience grows and/or your circumstances change. That's what happened in our household, and our children left the school system when they were nine, seven, and four.

The purpose of this book is to help you understand some of the basic principles behind unschooling—a style of homeschooling. Home-schooling generally encompasses methods of educating children in lieu of school. Often it means the children's education is dictated by the parents instead of by teachers, typically using purchased curricula or parent-designed unit studies. Then what is unschooling? Unschooling is, at its most basic, about learning without a curriculum, without a teacher-centred environment, but sometimes the concept is easier to define by what it's not. It's not school-at-home, a re-creation of the school environment with a low student-teacher ratio around the kitchen table. And it's not about leaving your kids to fend for themselves, far from it. It *is* about creating a different kind of learning environment for your children. An environment based on the understanding that humans learn best when they are interested and engaged, and when they are personally involved and motivated. Creating an environment conducive to real learning is very difficult if someone else—parent, teacher, or curriculum developer—is dictating what a person should be learning at any given time. But drop that outside control over the child and learning truly comes naturally. As the late John Holt (1983, 293), educator and unschooling advocate, notes so succinctly, "Fish swim, birds fly; man thinks and learns."

> *As parents, whether you choose public, private, or alternative school, homeschooling or unschooling, the act of making a conscious, well-informed choice regarding your child's learning environment is a crucial step.*

In addition, once you experience unschooling, you realize that there is much more to it than just dropping curriculum. It becomes a learning lifestyle—one where parents and children together enjoy exploring their interests and passions, learning along the way; one that evolves to inform your outlook on just about any situation that arises. Some like to call it *life learning* because what you are doing is learning through living. It revitalizes your relationships with your children. You will come to see that learning is often handicapped when confined to a classroom and a curriculum, but exciting and ubiquitous when children are given the freedom to explore their world. And soon you begin to glimpse the true nature of unschooling unfolding: living joyfully and passionately as a family, and building lifelong relationships in an environment where your children are free to discover and to grow into the people they were born to be.

Unschooling is a unique process for each family, and for each child. That may be why explaining unschooling is so straightforward and so difficult at the same time; the implications of that simple phrase *learning without a curriculum* are profound and life changing. This book is about exploring the ideas — the paradigm shifts — that will help you understand unschooling.

Learning about Learning

You take advantage of a quiet moment and call your best friend for some adult conversation. After a brief exchange of pleasantries you both sink into some serious conversation. Sharing with her your yearning to learn to sew, she promptly encourages you,

"Take a class!"

I'd like to share, up front, a few thoughts about how you might approach this book. As a first step, pay attention to the learning process that you are going through as you learn more about unschooling, as you read this and other books, browse websites, or meet up with other unschoolers. Use part of your mind to watch yourself objectively. Ask yourself how much you remember from your school career. Ask yourself how you prefer to learn day-to-day things now. The answers will help you to understand the learning process itself and to be open to seeing it in your children. How are you learning about unschooling?

Let's take an example. What are your options if you decide you want to learn how to edit your digital home videos? There are lots of ways to approach it. You could sign up for a class in your area. You could do a bit of research and choose some software, or download a demo and start playing around with it. Maybe you like to read through the user's manual before you get started, or just reference it when you are trying to figure out something specific. You could search for online help videos or support forums for that software. Maybe you know someone who has already done this and you could ask them to show you how to get started. There are many ways to learn something; a class is just one of them. Which ways work best for you?

What I learned about myself when I was a computer program developer, was that the classes I took (at the behest of my employer) were one of the least helpful ways for me to learn a programming language. The first day of a course was often useful, showing me around the software interface and introducing me to the basics of the language syntax, but the rest of the week I was often bored to frustration while programming answers to made-up sample exercises that were inevitably not much use outside the classroom. The real learning started once I got back to the office and started applying it to real-life business situations. With manuals strewn around my desk, I'd likely join an online forum or two to read through others' questions or post my own as needed, check out online programming tutorial sites, all the while making progress on what I was actually trying to accomplish. And if I didn't use the language soon after, either personally or at work, what I did pick up during the course was soon all but lost. So learning things as I come up against them in my life, as they help me accomplish something I'm striving toward, has served me very well.

This book will take you from the ideas behind unschooling through the extension of these ideas into day-to-day living. It is key to understand that unschooling is not just a different set of rules to live by. You can decide you don't like the school rules (written *and* unwritten) and you want something different for your family, but if you interpret the unschooling ideas presented here as just another set of rules and implement them without thought and awareness, life will most likely feel out of control for your whole family. Don't just skim through the ideas, as logical as they may seem on the surface. Really live with them. Let them percolate in the back of your mind as you go about your day. Recall your own learning experiences, in school and out, and see how they compare. It will take work on your part to deeply understand these concepts and bring them into the everyday life of your family, but it will be truly rewarding.

And one other note, if you are coming to unschooling from negative school experiences for you or your child, try to take any negative energy that you have and focus it on learning more about unschooling. It can be challenging to work through negative experiences, but that energy is wasted if it's focused on the past. Use it to help you learn and move forward. The reasons for choosing unschooling will change over time as you learn more and gain more experience seeing your kids learning and growing. As negative school experiences fade in your memory, more lasting and positive reasons to unschool will blossom. One day you'll look up from the book you're reading or the game you're enjoying with your children and it will hit you: you are unschooling!

IDEA ONE: REAL LEARNING

Let's take moment to look at the word *paradigm.* According to the Canadian Oxford Dictionary Second Edition it means "an example or pattern followed; a typical instance." There are common ideas in our society today that are held up as models for parenting and the business of dispensing childhood education. Moving to unschooling means examining these mainstream ideas to see how well they hold up in our lives, how well they serve us as a family. In *Free to Learn* I examine the five mainstream ideas I found most wanting as they applied to our lives. I underwent a paradigm shift with each of these ideas, "a fundamental change in approach," (Canadian Oxford Dictionary) that made sense to me, better described our lives, and helped me to more fully understand the principles behind unschooling.

Unschooling Paradigm ~ Learning is best defined by the learner.

Mainstream Paradigm: Children need to be taught. For learning to happen it needs to be directed by a teacher and measured through tests to prove success. Learning is defined by a teacher.

Paradigm Shift: Instead of looking at learning from a teacher's point of view, look at it from the learner's point of view. Real learning is best defined by the learner precisely because it can only take place *in* the learner, regardless of any teaching being done *around* the learner.

At first it may seem like a small shift of focus, looking through the learner's eyes instead of the teacher's—almost semantics—but this shift is the key to observing real learning. How do we get there?

Learning versus Teaching

The high school teacher stands at the front of the room. Noticing that there are only a couple minutes left in the class, he quickly wraps up his sentence and puts down the chalk. He notes that a number of students are busy with other things: doodling on scrap paper, twirling pencils, chatting quietly with their neighbours. He sighs, knowing they had not been paying attention to his explanation of photosynthesis. "Remember the test next week. It will cover Chapters 4 and 5, but not the section on the Calvin cycle; we'll cover that next month if we have time. Be sure you can describe the formula for photosynthesis!" The students that hear him dutifully write down the test hints. They all begin to gather their belongings. They wait impatiently for the bell to ring so they can chat freely for a couple minutes before trekking to their next class.

He was definitely teaching—but were the students learning? Did they understand the process he was trying to describe? Will they remember it? Does being in the presence of teaching ensure that learning is taking place? I think the vast majority of us can remember similar situations we were in where the answers were no. Whether teachers like it or not, the students themselves are completely in control of whether learning is happening.

During the next week, the majority of the students spend varying amounts of time studying Chapters 4 and 5 (but not the Calvin cycle section because why bother, it's not on the test), trying to memorize the photosynthesis formula, trying to guess whether they will have to label the parts of a chloroplast cell on the test. Some will memorize everything just in case, others will guess well and get a decent mark this time (or not), still others don't like biology and accordingly don't put much effort into memorizing facts they don't think they'll ever use in real life. The tests are returned and some are pleased, some are disappointed, others are indifferent. They all move on.

It's a month later and the teacher announces the next test covering Chapters 6, 7, and 8, but not the Calvin cycle as they didn't have time to cover it. The cycle starts again. But what if on test day he hands out the previous test instead? How well do you think the students would do?

Is memorizing really learning? Does memorizing a process mean that it is understood? That it will be remembered in the long-term? If it is forgotten a month later, was it really learned? These are great questions to ask yourself.

Teaching is about the relationship between two people, teacher and student. The goal is that the student learns a particular piece of information or skill from the teacher. Since learning is the goal, isn't it best to define the outcome from that standpoint? It is much more relevant to observe the result from the student's point of view; from the learning, rather than from the teaching. When describing your daughter's newest achievement, tying her shoelaces, it is more accurate to say *she learned* than to say *I taught her*. You may well have shown her various ways to tie her shoes and on different occasions, but at the moment she was ready to put it all together she learned how to tie her shoes. *She learned* is also more accurate than *she taught herself*. She didn't know how before, so how could she teach it to herself? She learned.

For the next while, every time you find yourself using or thinking the word *teach*, take a moment to rethink the situation and substitute the word *learn*. You'll begin to see life from the learner's point of view and that's great because that's where all the action is.

What Is Learning?

Gathering the dishes on the coffee table to take back to the kitchen, a commercial on TV catches your attention: "Did you know children can lose up to two and a half months of learning over the summer?"

Let's talk about what learning means. Is it memorizing and recalling facts and methods? If Tom memorizes a set of facts, recites it for a test, and receives a good mark, does this mean he learned that information? A good mark is how schools typically define successful learning because pen-and-paper tests are the easiest way to measure the progress of individuals in large groups. But if Tom can no longer remember that information a couple months later, did he really learn it? From the school's point of view, an *A* on a test or report card is still an *A* two months later; so yes, he did.

What about from the learner's point of view? What if a couple months later he can no longer regurgitate that particular fact, solve that geometry problem, or recall the meaning of that Shakespearean soliloquy he can still (almost) recite? It means he can't take that piece of information about the world with him and connect it to other interesting bits he may come across. It may be sitting in memory somewhere but it isn't connected to anything meaningful for the learner. When the viewpoint is the learner living in the world, then it follows that he hasn't really learned that piece of knowledge. It is of no real use to him because it's not an accessible piece of information about his world; it is at best a random factoid.

Real learning occurs when information is understood and remembered. Understanding results from being able to make sense of a piece of information by seeing how it fits into the world, how it connects to other bits of information to make a more complete picture in the learner's mind. And understanding makes it more memorable—like a puzzle piece that has fallen into place and become integrated into the learner's knowledge base.

There are a couple other related mainstream beliefs about learning I'd like to examine while we're here. One belief is about learning certain things at certain ages. This belief is perpetuated by school because of the assembly-line nature of the educational system. Curricula are useful tools to ensure that by the end of their schooling career each student has touched upon the topics deemed necessary. Without that guideline Mr. Smith, Tom's third grade teacher, and Ms. Jones, his fifth grade teacher, might both choose to teach medieval history because they each find it fascinating, while Tom misses out on pioneer times altogether!

But curricula are artificial constructs independent of learning itself; they are predominately for the management of masses of students. With unschooling, this need to learn certain things at certain ages is irrelevant and the child is free to learn things as they come up in life. The focus is not on learning what someone has deemed they *need* to know by the time they are ten or thirteen or eighteen (and graduating into the real world). The focus for unschoolers is on living in the real world every day and learning things as needed to accomplish the real and meaningful goals in front of them.

If Tom becomes interested in medieval history after seeing the movie *A Knight's Tale,* or pioneer times after visiting the local pioneer village, he can delve into it right then, regardless of his age. He can learn about jousting when he encounters jousting. Does it matter if he is seven or twelve or twenty-one or forty-two when that happens? What if he never happens to come across jousting? Would that hamper his ability to live a fulfilling life? I certainly don't think so.

The second belief is the focus on *what* to learn, instead of *how* to learn. There are two challenges here. One is that the body of useful knowledge needed to live in the information age of the twenty-first century is changing so rapidly that school curricula can't keep up. Significant portions of the skill set held by typical high school students may well be obsolete within a decade after graduation.

The other challenge is accommodating different learning styles. This is a daunting task in the highly structured school environment. Those students that don't learn well in the typical classroom environment are regarded as unintelligent and many carry that judgment well into their adult lives. People don't realize that the issue was really that the typical classroom setup was not conducive to *how* they learn best.

In contrast, the unschooling child is free to pursue and learn things they are interested in, keeping pace with the changing skill set in their areas of interest while along the way instinctively figuring out how they prefer to learn: hands-on tinkering, reading, watching, listening, or more typically, a fluid combination of some or all of those styles. Discovering and understanding *how* we learn best is a skill that will serve us well throughout our lives. Learning can easily continue beyond school age, if one remains curious. To me, this is the underlying issue being addressed by futurist Alvin Toffler (1998, 271), as he quotes psychologist Herbert Geurjoy, "Tomorrow's illiterate will not be the man who can't read; he will be the man who has not learned how to learn."

Building a View of the World

Lauren accepts her rolled up diploma and dutifully shakes the principal's hand, then lines up with her fellow graduates. As soon as the formal ceremony ends, she and her friends then break out of their serious demeanour, share high-fives and hugs, and shout, "Woohoo! No more classes ever! Real world, here I come!"

Now that we're focusing on the learning instead of the teaching and on the long-term learning connections made by the learner, let's see how it all comes together. What does it look like over time?

Each person is building a unique view of the world. That view includes how they fit into the world, how they interact with the world, and how the world works—scientifically, mathematically, artistically, and historically. All the bits and pieces of the world are not as independent from each other as school subjects imply. Those pieces of information connect together to create our environment, our society. Instead of having a goal of graduation for our children, let's look beyond: They are living in the world. That is what we'd like to help them do.

The commonly held ideal behind school is to teach children a set of skills and a body of general knowledge that will allow them to function in the real world when they graduate. Do you remember when you were in school and sometimes you wondered why you would need to learn a certain thing? The answer was usually some version of, "You'll need to know it when you're older and out in the real world. Trust me."

In school, the learning is often disconnected from the living, even as the curriculum tries hard to imitate it. The bigger picture of how a piece of information is useful to the student and how it connects to their world (thus making it understandable and memorable) is often glossed over quickly or missing entirely because it can be different for each student. The teacher doesn't have enough time to understand and explain to each student how each piece of knowledge uniquely connects to their personal existing knowledge base. This lack of time means teachers must generalize and assume every student's existing

> *If you're ready to embrace life and eager to share its wonder with your children, life in the real world is much bigger and more exciting than school can contain within its four walls.*

knowledge base is the same: the school's curricula up to this point.

Because of the masses of students that must be moved through the system, the curricula are based on a generalized view of the *real world*. How does one define the real world? Just as there is no perfectly typical person, there is no perfectly typical real world that every student will enter upon graduation. The knowledge and skills that a person needs to know to successfully navigate their life varies widely depending on their interests, on what career and life goals they choose to pursue, not to mention a host of other personal factors. What they really need to prepare for is their piece of the world, the part of the world they will choose to inhabit.

Unschooling children (not bound by a standard curriculum) are able to delve more deeply into the areas of the world that interest them, those areas that they are more likely to be involved in as they get older. Sure, there may be a set of basic information and skills that almost everyone may want to have, but that is because those skills are basic to our society. As such, unschooling children living day-to-day with their families will come across them too. Do you worry that they might not encounter a skill they really need to know? Think about that for a moment. If they don't come across it during their day-to-day lives, is it really a necessary skill? Why? Maybe they just haven't encountered it yet, and will pick it up easily enough when it comes up, or maybe they never will bump into it. The point is that there is no start or end to learning; it can happen at any time, at any age, whenever the need to attain the skill or knowledge arises.

One proviso though, unschooling won't work well if you actively avoid having your family interact with the world, with life. Shutting out the world rather than embracing it will limit your children's opportunities to learn, maybe to the point where school is more connected to the world than home is. Inhibiting their exploration of the world around them is not helpful or supportive of learning.

But if you're ready to embrace life and eager to share its wonder with your children, life in the real world is much bigger and more exciting than school can contain within its four walls. You can help your children explore the world, encourage their fascination with all the pieces that catch their interest, and help them build their own unique view. This is one of the best ways to encourage a lifelong love of learning.

Deschooling

Natalie wakes up early, excited to grab a few minutes to continue building her fort in the backyard before she has to leave for school. As she quickly eats breakfast, you remind her she has a quiz this morning at school and she needs to study instead. You know she's disappointed so you remind her she can get back to it after school. Natalie shakes her head sadly, "No, I've got band practice after school today. I guess it'll have to wait until after dinner." You have more bad news for her. "No, you have to finish your science homework tonight. Maybe tomorrow."

It takes time to move from a teacher-centred, structured view of learning to a learner-centred one. This period of decompression and change of focus is often called deschooling. The guideline for this process is one month for every year of schooling— whether in a school building or school-at-home. But remember, don't stress if this process takes longer than you expect. The whole family will need time to relax and adjust to life without the imposed structure of a school timetable.

What does one do while deschooling? It's a wonderful time to discover your children's interests and rediscover the joy of learning. Enjoy your children's interests alongside them and help them dig into them as deeply as they'd like. Seeing them learn about things they are interested in is inspiring to watch. Leave them to unwind without the pressure of any expectations. Join them often, just to hang out together. Pick up some interests of your own and share them if asked. Discover things you're all interested in and pursue them together. Give them something new that you think they'd be interested in; not something you wish they would be interested in, but something you truly think they'd enjoy. Then don't be bitter or discouraged if they pass on it. Brainstorm together things they'd like to do at home and out in the community. Some great ideas for deschooling (and living!) activities include watching movies, visiting the local attractions (science centre, museum, paintball field, water park, conservation parks, mall, ice cream parlour, pizza joint, zoo, and pioneer village, just to name a few), playing a week-long Monopoly game, making playdough, swimming, hiking, fishing, skiing, building a huge Lego town, beating that video game, putting together a thousand-piece puzzle. I bet you can come up with a great list unique to your family. Have fun together!

> *What does one do while deschooling? It's a wonderful time to discover your children's interests and rediscover the joy of learning.*

Focus on really *being* with your kids; not just in body, but in mind as well (that is, don't have part of your brain thinking about what you're going to make for dinner) or you may miss something fascinating. If you like to write, maybe now is a great time to start a journal. Not a schoolish journal with subject dividers like reading, math, science—those topics will make it difficult for you to see *all* the learning that's happening.

How about one that chronicles everyday life in general? Write down what they get up to, what their favourite activities are, what they chat about, what interesting comments they make, and so on. When you read it over after a few months, you will see their personal learning patterns emerge, how some interests led to others, how their activities are developing, and their overall growth as people.

In your free time, continue reading and thinking critically, and learning about unschooling. Parents are usually the ones who have been in the school system the longest and thus have the most deschooling to do. Analyze your own school experiences: Do you remember everything you were taught? Did you learn better when you were interested in the subject? Did the structure of school interfere with your learning? Think about what you've read here so far about learning in general. What is the real purpose of learning things? What does real learning look like? Is it necessary to learn certain things at certain ages? How do you best like to learn? Is it ever too late to learn something?

A common worry is whether there's a distinct window for your child to learn a second language, and if you miss it, you have somehow failed them. It may be easier to learn another language at a younger age, but it's not too late to learn it when one is older;

people do it all the time. If a child is interested in learning another language when they're young, have fun with it. (I don't mean asking a three year old if they want to learn French. Put on a French TV show, sing some French songs, play with French words.) But if they aren't interested, a parent insisting a child learn a second language just because it may come more easily and maybe someday they'll want to speak it, can damage the relationship. It also sends the message that the parent should be defining what the child learns. It becomes an *I know better than you*, or, *for your own good* situation, and where does that stop? The key is the learner's interest.

> *Sometimes you'll find you need to use your energy to stay out of their way and watch learning blossom from a distance.*

A paradigm shift doesn't happen overnight. You think and observe and analyze until the process culminates in a shift that reaches all the corners of your mind and rings loudly with its truth in your unique view of the world. Answering the kinds of questions posed in this chapter for yourself will help you figure out what real learning means to you.

Unschooling is not about just getting rid of school; it's about replacing school with a different kind of environment for learning, one that is more supportive of how people learn naturally (the way your children first learned to walk and talk). All that energy you employed to get them up in the morning, make their lunches, get them off to school, help them with their homework, etc., you can now put to great use building relationships with them, helping them pursue their interests, and bringing them together with interesting things in the world. But stay responsive to their feedback, spoken and unspoken. It's not about being assertive and insistent with your support. Sometimes you'll find you need to use your energy to stay out of their way and watch learning blossom from a distance.

The day deschooling *ends* and unschooling *begins* won't be lit up in bright lights—there's no magic moment. Life will just continue with the wonderful rhythm you've found. You'll see all the learning that's happening every day and eventually you'll look back and realize, "Hey, I think we're unschooling!"

IDEA TWO: FOLLOWING THEIR INTERESTS

Unschooling Paradigm ~ Learning is

everywhere.

Mainstream Paradigm: Educational experts should define what and how children learn.

Paradigm Shift: Learning need not be defined as exclusively occurring in classrooms, during school hours, with those of school age. It can be found everywhere, at anytime, and can happen at any age.

We've talked about how you do not need a curriculum to lay out what needs to be learned before you can live successfully in the real world. And instead, how children can learn what they need to by living in the real world. People (and again, children are people) enjoy learning things that are useful to them now, and they learn best when they are interested and engaged.

Where Is Learning Found?

Glancing at your watch you wonder where the afternoon has gone—you have a load of laundry to wash and dinner to get started soon. A bit ahead of you on the trail, George brings you out of your thoughts. "Mom! Come see the marks on this tree!" You quickly catch up and lean over to look at the trunk. "I think those were made by a beaver." "Really? What was it trying to do?" You answer matter-of-factly, "It was trying to cut down the tree and use it to build its home in the river." "So cool! Let's go to the river and look for them!" Straightening up, you turn toward the parking lot. You can see the excitement in his eyes but you're tired and want to get home and get dinner on the table. "Not today,

George. Maybe next time."

So if we don't follow a curriculum, where is learning found? We find it in the living, in the world. Let's look at that in more detail.

Schools realize they are preparing their students for the magical day they graduate into the mysterious real world. They try to replicate it with play food and play money and play stock markets, with pictures of real places and simplified science experiments. Then there are the word problems that try to simulate real-life scenarios, (Your mother gives you $5.00 and the toy you want to buy costs $12.50 ...) and some that aren't so relevant, (If train A leaves the station traveling east at a speed of X and train B is traveling west ...). They try to push this knowledge into the learner in hopes that it is absorbed and understood well enough for the student to apply it in the real world once they graduate.

Mainstream educators also realize that more learning happens when the child is happily engaged. One outcome is the recent rise in edutainment software, a mixture of educational and entertainment genres. Edutainment software is often more fun than a worksheet, but the concepts used in the games are still removed from life and are now superficially embedded in a storyline. The student is still left to figure out how shooting a balloon with a 12 on it when he sees 3X4 written on the billboard in the desert applies in the real world; it still focuses on teaching the skill versus its real-life connection.

Instead, how about needing to move twelve spaces after rolling double sixes in Monopoly? The player soon discovers that moving two spaces six times, or three spaces four times makes the counting, and the game, go faster. Or noticing that to quickly choose a dozen muffins at the local bakery it helps to ask for three each of your four favourite varieties. Or observing that when you receive six status upgrades in your video game after a boss fight, that with three team members you can award them equally by giving every member two upgrades. These are real-life situations where multiplication is a useful tool, and therefore, the knowledge is understood and remembered.

In school, the focus is on learning the skills: learning to read is in itself a goal, learning the multiplication tables, learning the capital cities. But stuck within the confines of the school's four walls, kids find it hard to understand why they might want to learn many of these things. Those subjects are disconnected from their life. And without the connection to real-life goals, learning these skills is all the more difficult. They need something to connect it to, some way for it to make sense in their world and with that gain understanding and real learning.

For example, at our house learning to read is not a goal. But as my daughter immersed herself in the world of Harry Potter, she learned a lot about reading along the way. We don't have learning percentages as a goal. But as my son worked to create a well-rounded party that could defeat the final boss in his video game, an understanding of percentages and data management was pretty crucial. This learning is really incidental to the goal—just stepping stones, something to figure out along the way—but it is real learning; it makes sense in their world and has purpose. And they truly enjoy it because it helps them accomplish their goal. Learning is fun!

Those are a couple of real-life examples. But do you wonder how your child will encounter the need or wish to learn a wide range of things in their day-to-day lives?

Think about that. What if your child just lives in the real world with you instead of learning from simulated life in school? Think of all the real and meaningful learning she would experience. What if she goes grocery shopping with you and checks out the real produce for sale that day? Comparison shops between brands? What if she has $5 allowance in her pocket and she wants a toy that costs more; you could discuss with her how much more she would need to save to afford it or how she could borrow from you. That's real life and learning. Maybe later you drive to the local park and play around by the river. You watch the water flow and the fish rest in the twists and turns of the river, and you consider the design of a beaver dam. Maybe she's a bit older, and searching YouTube she finds some great videos on playing guitar; maybe she records an interesting Discovery Channel series on the one hundred greatest discoveries in science. And while browsing through the local library, she finds a book series that delights her. Maybe she enjoys the series of art classes put on by a local artist. At this time in history, there is so much information readily available in the world; it is no longer only available in the classroom, dispensed by a teacher.

Another interesting thing to note is how different learning looks outside of school. The plodding and relentless nature of curriculum makes learning appear to happen steadily—chapter one this week, chapter two the next. But real learning often happens in a seemingly erratic pattern of fits and starts. Progress seems stymied for a while, then a stubborn connection is finally made, cascading rapidly through any number of quick learning connections until another challenging question comes into focus and slows us down again for a while. Real learning is not as systematic as a curriculum outline would have us believe.

Do you wonder about more advanced topics as your child gets older? There are a couple considerations here. First, older children are likely adept now at finding and learning information they are interested in pursuing. They are also more likely to feel comfortable exploring new environments related to their areas of interests, such as the local photography club or rocket-building group where they'll find more experienced people who love to share their knowledge and enthusiasm. Maybe they'll find a mentor to help them delve even deeper into their passion.

I recently received an email asking about the future of my son, Joseph, and his interest in video games. This question touches a common concern that people have when they are first learning about unschooling: "I am curious, is he planning on going to college? Game development degrees require math courses such as Calculus II and III. As an unschooled student, won't he be at a major disadvantage in college, when he needs to take these advanced courses?"

The specific answer for my son, at this moment, is that he is interested in the story aspect of game development, not programming. But this doesn't really address the underlying unschooling idea that learning can happen whenever there is interest, so I answered more fully.

Even if he were interested in programming, we still wouldn't consider him to be at a major disadvantage. There are many ways to get into the gaming industry without college, but if he were to choose college, catching up with the math curriculum would not likely be the overwhelming ordeal it may sound like. Even though he hasn't taken formal math classes since he left school, he has definitely encountered math concepts. And with a lifelong view of learning we don't look at starting at the beginning to learn something new as a disadvantage, but as a choice. He could work through some math books on his own, take a summer class, or a remedial course in college. The time others have spent learning what they know (say, a high school math curriculum), he's spent learning something else that makes up his knowledge base. It's not a competition with others and time is not lost, just used at his preference.

Those are two important concepts to internalize. There is no right and wrong time to learn something when learning is seen as a lifelong endeavour; learn it when you want or need the knowledge. And there is no behind or ahead in learning. Comparing marks or knowledge against others is not a measure of personal learning and is irrelevant to the learner if the goal is

> *Real learning often happens in a seemingly erratic pattern of fits and starts. Progress seems stymied for a while, then a stubborn connection is finally made, cascading rapidly through any number of quick learning connections until another challenging question comes into focus and slows us down again for a while.*

expanding their own knowledge base.

Now let's shift. Do you value one kind of learning over another? Do you think reading about something is superior to watching a TV show about it? Is visiting an exhibition on the topic better than reading about it? How about participating in a group interested in the same topic? Why?

Let's say the topic of interest is medieval times. You could visit the library and pick up some books, ranging from picture books to history texts. You could search through upcoming listings on satellite or cable to see if anything related is coming up. You could search DVD services for documentaries or movies depicting that time period. You could visit the local museum for exhibits, or plan a fun weekend into the nearest city with an extensive display. In the summer you could dress up in period costume and visit a Renaissance Faire to dive more deeply into that world. There are so many possibilities. Bits and pieces of medieval-times knowledge can be had from all of these sources, and more. What if your child is not interested in reading the books you found but can't get enough of the documentaries? Are they still learning interesting things about medieval times? Yes. What if they love the books and the museum, but don't want to dress up or visit the local Faire? What if they really just want to fashion their own lance and run around jousting with friends? Still learning? Absolutely.

What your child is drawn to pursuing and learning is what is making meaningful connections for them at this time. And that is real learning — knowledge that is understood and remembered. The stuff they choose to forgo? Maybe it was the presentation style, maybe it was the content; it doesn't matter. What they pass up now, your child may be drawn to later, a week from now or five years from now. Or maybe never, if it doesn't again cross their radar, or pique their interest.

Learning is found everywhere. And all types of learning are of value to the learner—connections are made regardless of how they are sparked or the vehicle through which they are delivered. Now let's look at how these connections work.

Connections Create the Web of Learning

Isabella loves her birthday! She's thrilled to be making her list with you, "I want a princess dress, and a wand, and a princess storybook, and a frog puppet. Oh! And a tea set, and a toy castle, and a princess colouring book! I'd love the new princess movie. And a Prince Charming doll!" You laugh, "Is there any-thing that you'd like for your birthday that isn't princess related?"

Connections are the thrill of learning; they are how we build our own view of the world. How do those learning connections weave together? Let's take a couple examples and see where they could lead.

A classic example for us is The Simpsons TV show. Many parents are wary of letting their children watch since the attitudes to adults seem quite disrespectful. But there is so much there to spark conversations and learning!

When my children were younger it was the plot that they enjoyed most. I recall watching with my kids an episode that parodied Hamlet. Soon after we were watching the Reduced Shakespeare Company's DVD The Complete Works of William Shakespeare (abridged) and when they were doing their version of Hamlet the kids were busy relating it to The Simpsons' version ("Tales from the Public Domain"). One of the "Treehouse of Horror" episodes included a skit based on Edgar Allan Poe's poem, "The Raven". My daughter found this fascinating and the next week she bought a book collection of some of Poe's work and eagerly read through it. As they got older they began to catch more of the underlying social commentary, sparking more discussions from the portrayal of girls in media to the meaning of Christmas to taking care of our parents as they age. The show is a smorgasbord of life topics and we enjoy it together.

For others, their interest in The Simpsons could lead to an interest in animation, or drawing, or comedy. For some it has lead to writing about the philosophical questions raised in the show (Irwin 2001). Any interest has the potential to expand in many directions, which is what makes the web metaphor so apt.

Another example of learning connections is my younger son's karate. Michael started with one class a week, but as his interest solidified, he chose more and more classes (currently up to four nights a week). Japanese is often used at the dojo—for counting, for naming the different moves—and that has sparked an interest in learning more Japanese. He has delved into websites and has bought a Nintendo DS game about learning the language. He has explored different types of physical training to increase his strength and endurance and he attends additional workshops to further his skills. Michael's interest in karate has also led to an interest in learning how to eat in a more healthy way. It's not just karate and it's not just about physical activity either.

Being out in the world doing things they are interested in—along with the freedom to pursue any related threads they discover—creates an environment in which real learning thrives. It is exciting and fun! Think about this in relation to your own learning. What was the last thing you learned outside school? What interest have you pursued with gusto? Did you find yourself following interesting tangents as you explored the topic? It's likely you did. When you were surfing for information on the internet, did you find an interesting website or blog, and then follow an intriguing link to another blog, then maybe another and another, learning all sorts of bits and pieces along the way? It's not a coincidence that they call it the World Wide Web. Just as the internet is a web of virtual connections (links and search results), our personal learning is a web of connections in our mind.

As you move toward unschooling and observe your child making these connections, as you see their connected view and understanding of the world growing, you begin to trust that learning is still happening, even if you sometimes don't explicitly see or understand the connections your child is making.

At this point I hope you're starting to get comfortable with the idea that learning is everywhere; that bringing your child into contact with the world (versus trying to bring some semblance of the world into the classroom) helps build meaningful connections. Exploring together will support your child's real learning.

But what if your child is not particularly interested in getting out in the world and exploring all sorts of different things? What if right now they have one interest, a passionate interest that they prefer to explore to the exclusion of others? Does this hinder unschooling? How will they learn the various skills and basic information that will help them live in the world as they grow older with such a seemingly narrow focus? Let's investigate these questions by looking deeper at some real-life examples.

Embracing Passions

"Mom! This figure would be perfect standing by the tracks in my town! Can we get it? Please?" You smile grimly—you'd tried walking quickly past the store display, knowing Christopher would ask for yet another accessory if he noticed the toys. "Not today, Christopher. All you do is play with your trains! Don't you get bored? Why don't we play catch outside when we get home?" Christopher is disappointed, but not surprised. He knows you don't much approve of his love of trains.

It may seem counterintuitive at first, but even focused interests open up the world for exploration. I saw it in action in my own family.

When my two eldest children were younger, they both dove deep into ostensibly singular interests. Instead of trying to coax them out of their realms in hopes of them being well-rounded, I joined them to try to discover the joy they were experiencing. Why weren't they getting bored? How involved could playing video games really be? Sure, the Harry Potter books were great, but what more could there be to enjoy after reading them a few times? After a while, I was astonished to discover the incredible breadth of learning I found! I was inspired to draw up a connections map or web, for each of their passions that laid out the learning connections I'd seen in those few months. Lissy's Harry Potter exploration included threads weaving into reading, writing, research, crafts, religion, mythology, computers, movies, and music, while Joseph's video game explorations wove their way into math, reading, writing, mythology, Japanese language, game development, and social and personal development. There were probably more that I didn't catch, but this was enough to convince me that even diving deep into a singular passion allowed incredible access to the world. Here are the two maps I created in 2006.

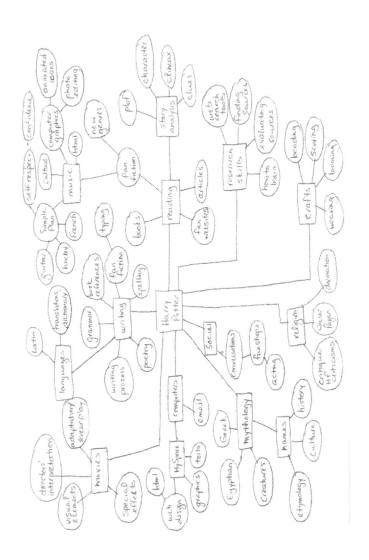

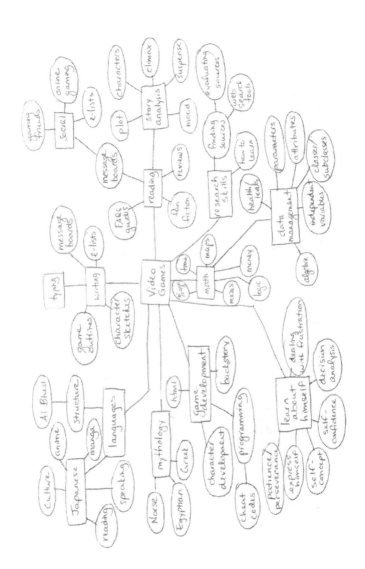

Video Games (central concept)

Reading
- Story analysis
  - characters
  - climax
  - suspense
  - Plot
  - mood
- Social
  - anime gaming
  - e-lists
  - gaming friends
- message boards
- reviews
- Fan fiction
- FAQs guides

Research skills
- evaluating sources
- web search tools
- finding sources
- how to learn
- health ideas

Data management
- parameters
- attributes
- classes
- subclasses
- independent variables
- algebra

Math
- geography time
- map
- money
- maps
- logic

Writing
- typing
- message boards
- e-lists
- game storylines
- character sketches

Languages
- AI Bhd
- structure
- anime
- manga
- Japanese
  - culture
  - reading
  - speaking

Mythology
- Norse
- Egyptian
- Greek

Game Development
- Atari
- backstory
- character development
- programming
- cheat codes

Learn about himself
- dealing with frustration
- decision analysis
- self-confidence
- self-concept
- express himself
- patience/perseverance

It's important to give your child the freedom to explore the threads they discover as they dig into their passion. When talking with them, it may seem to be video games (or Harry Potter, or trains, or The Simpsons, or space, or dinosaurs) all the time, but through that filter they are picking up many new skills, making all sorts of interesting connections that are understood and remembered. And these are skills and connections that can be called upon in new situations. You can help these connections grow by sharing their enthusiasm and bringing related things into their world for them to discover. Being involved with them as they explore means you will see the web of connections growing, see real learning happening.

If worry that they seem so focused causes you to interfere with their exploration by pushing them to pursue other topics, your actions may well have the opposite effect. They will probably spend their required time at those other activities wishing instead that they were busy with their passion. Not only are they not learning much from the new activity because they are unhappy and distracted, the time that they would have spent learning more widely through their passion is lost.

> *No one method of learning is superior to another, except to an individual. Truly, learning is everywhere.*

Looking back now, I think my children's passionate explorations of their interests led them far and wide precisely because they were young and there was so much new and interesting stuff in the world for them to learn. That's in stark contrast to their few years in school where rote learning was disconnected from their interests and as a result, was quite boring and arduous. This learning was exciting!

Joseph's and Lissy's exploration of their passions touched many of the basic skills (reading, writing, math, web skills, and so on) that now help them live so comfortably in the real world day-to-day. Interestingly, delving into their passions now is much more pointed—much more about depth than breadth. There is less of a need to cast the net wider because they already possess the basic skills and knowledge in those general areas. Lissy's current interest in photography is deep and wide, but at this time is mostly contained within the artistic realm rather than the technical or business sides; she often spends hours each day deep in the work of creating and editing images, or pouring over photos in magazines, or surfing the web for information and inspiration. Sure, if she hadn't already learned the basics about computers, she'd be picking them up now as part of learning image—manipulation software; or if she wasn't already web savvy, she would be well on her way through using photo—sharing websites; or if she wasn't already sporting good web research skills, she'd be honing them now as she combs the web for photography information;

or if she hadn't already delved deeply into writing as part of her Harry Potter exploration, she'd be developing fine writing skills now through communicating with other photographers.

This pattern of real learning, of reaching out to gather skills when needed, is not age based as so many of us have discovered outside the age-dominant regime of school. The process of real learning is individual and based on each child's unique personality and internal readiness. No one skill or personality is necessary or even advantageous for living and learning in the world, even reading.

Every child's unique combination of personality and skills means that how they learn will also be unique to them:

> - some children are capable of reading at a young age and some not until much later, but that doesn't slow them down outside the classroom because information in the real world comes in so many shapes and sizes;

> - some children love spending time in big groups of kids, others in small groups, still others with just their family or mostly on their own;

> - some will explore the world through their most passionate interest; others will

discover its joys through various ongoing hobbies.

But one thing is certain: free to learn, children in all these overlapping groups will gather knowledge and pick up skills in ways that work for them. They may prefer to learn through books or magazines (read by themselves or by others); TV, movies, or documentaries; mentors or interested peers; hands-on exploration; online websites, blogs, and podcasts; visits to related places close or far; and so forth. No one method of learning is superior to another, except to an individual. Truly, learning is everywhere.

So, now you're getting comfortable with the idea that learning can happen by living, and that following their interests will lead them to that learning. Next, how can we support our children as they explore the world?

IDEA THREE: CHOICES

Unschooling Paradigm ~ Choices are key to learning.

Mainstream Paradigm: Parents who make most of the decisions for their child are modeling the *right thing to do* so that their child will remember and make those same choices as a young adult and beyond.

Paradigm Shift: Instead of learning *what* choices to make, it's better to learn *how* to make informed choices.

Unschooling children are picking up skills and gathering information all the time, but at the same time they are learning how to navigate the world. How to make choices and decisions in both unique and everyday situations is a key life skill. How do we help them gain experience with this?

Judging Choices

It's a beautiful fall day and you are looking forward to going for a walk. Jeremy quickly pulls on his running shoes, dashes out the door, and shouts, "Come on, Mom!" Your smile falters as you notice his sweater still hanging on the hook, remembering the talk you gave him just yesterday about wearing it when he goes out in this cooler weather. As you walk through the door you say firmly, "Jeremy, get back here and put on your sweater!" A beat passes and you add, "NOW!" Running back he protests that he's not cold, but you insist. He does as he's told but his excitement has waned and the joyful stroll you envisioned has morphed into a determined march around the block accompanied by repeated moans about the

sweater, and you both head back inside.

You may think your child needs to wear a sweater out for a walk on this fall day, but only the child can really tell whether he'll feel best with or without it. He may well be warm enough without it because he's running ahead and back, or his body temperature naturally runs higher than yours right now. Absolutely offer a sweater if you think it seems cool out, but there's no need to insist; bring it along if you think he might change his mind. With the choice of a sweater available, he may decide to wear it after being outside for a while, or not. But he will have added a bit of real experience that will factor in next time he finds himself in similar circumstances. He's learning how to analyze situations and make choices.

One of the basic skills for anyone exploring the world and learning through living is making choices: What do I want to do today? Should I sign up for that interesting-sounding workshop? Do I want to take a bath or a shower? Eat a sandwich or a burger? Should I quit swimming lessons? Do I want to wade into the river or take the path through the trees?

Often, choices are rather basic, mostly personal preference, with no significant consequences one way or the other. But making those small choices is good preparation for when the bigger ones come along.

Helping your child gain experience in making choices entails a lot of trust from you, certainly at first. You can develop this trust in a couple of ways. One is to examine your thoughts surrounding choices. Spend some time reflecting on whether the same choice is necessarily right for everyone. Remember, your child is not just an extension of you. It's not hard to imagine that different choices in the same situation could work out well for different people, yet it's still pretty easy to fall into the trap of thinking that you know the best choice for another person: a spouse, a friend, or especially a child you love and want the best for. A second way to develop trust is through experience. We'll talk about that in a minute.

As part of pondering the idea of there being a range of suitable choices in similar situations, you will likely contemplate the inverse: if you believe your choice is the best choice, the only choice, where do you go from there? Is it helpful to manipulate others into seeing that your choice for them should be their choice as well? Thinking further you may begin to realize your judgment of the situation is tied up in your personal history; you really can't know everything about someone else's thoughts and goals, their emotional landscape, their physical reality. While you have their best interests at heart, you can't know for sure what the best choice is for them.

While developing this trust, it is important that you don't judge their choices, even implicitly. Real choice is lost if you even subtly manipulate them with a sigh or a certain look. Certainly discuss the options, but it's important that they feel free to follow their preference because people learn best from an experience when it is their own. If they are living someone else's choices, they are often learning something different. Can you recall a situation where this was true for you? Even as an adult, when you're told what to do, it is human nature to feel a twinge of rebellion, especially when you think there is a better choice. You may well do what you're told, but what you are likely thinking about and learning from is not the situation at hand, but rather your feelings toward the messenger—your boss, your coach, or your parent.

As I mentioned earlier, the other way you can learn to trust your child is through experience. Each time your child makes a considered choice that works out, you gain some experience. Each time your child makes a considered choice that wasn't the choice you'd advise and it still works out, you gain even more experience. And you trust a bit more. Then you see another choice work out, and another. Then you see a choice that didn't work out so well, and you notice your child incorporate that information into their next related decision. More learning in action. With experience, you become less fearful and more trusting of your child making their own choices. Eventually you and your child work out a harmonious relationship around choices where your input is thoughtfully considered by your child, and their decision is respectfully accepted by you.

Learning from Living

Kaylee runs to the sink to refill her teapot for the umpteenth time this afternoon. She giggles, "My teddy bears are thirsty again!" As you peel carrots you reply, "That's nice, Kaylee. Dinner will be ready soon. Don't forget you have to clean up before we eat." Twenty minutes later you tell her it's time to put her teddy bears away and come to the table for dinner. She cries, "No! I still want to play with them!" You remind her she agreed to put them away before dinner when you agreed to carry out her favourite stuffed bears. She sobs and pleads, but you hold firm to your agreement. She eventually joins the family at the dinner table, quietly picks at her food for a while, and asks to be excused.

Building on the awareness that choices are often personal preference, not right or wrong, and that subverting another person's choices often derails their learning, let's look more closely at how children learn from living their choices.

Most of the day-to-day decisions in a child's life may seem significant to the parent in the moment but in the bigger picture of childhood they are often inconsequential. To whom does it really matter if your child wears her favourite Halloween costume to the grocery store? In these moments, she has the opportunity to revel in the attention and delight of the other shoppers as they admire her princess gown, and to decide next time that she'd like a quiet trip and choose to forgo the costume. Or if she eats her favourite peanut butter sandwich for breakfast, lunch, and dinner this week? It gives her the time to discover when she's had her fill of peanut butter and would like to try something new. What if she sets up a tea party in the living room for her teddy bears and wants to keep it there to enjoy tea and dainty finger sandwiches for the next few days? After immersing herself in all the tea-related fun she can imagine, she eventually notices that she'd like a clean slate for her next creation. And she may well discover that a tidy room can be quite as exciting as a busy one.

As the parent, you can take a moment to look at the bigger picture and realize these are wonderful and exciting adventures to your child; more exciting to her than a clean living room would be to you. It's about giving the child the opportunity to discover these things on her timetable, as they have meaning for her, rather than on the parent's timetable, where they don't have meaning and the connections aren't made.

Let's take another look at my son's karate interest from the perspective of timing. Michael's interest in martial arts was evident for quite a while before he decided to try out classes at a dojo. When I first mentioned that he might enjoy karate classes he replied noncommittally and at least a year passed before he asked to go. At the time I offered, we discussed it a bit, and I left the choice to him.

Seeing how much he enjoys going to the dojo now does not mean that his choice to wait was wrong, nor does it mean that I should have cajoled or convinced him to try it back then. It was not a missed opportunity, he was simply not ready. If I had pushed him to go earlier, he may have ended up enjoying himself and continuing, but he may also have been turned off the sport itself because even though he was interested, he would be going at my behest, not directly from his own desire to explore karate. In fact, the dojo is a wonderful example of pursuing an interest when a person is ready; there are beginner white belts of all ages, from age four to over forty.

Experience in making the smaller choices in life while growing up has a number of wonderful benefits for children: they get to know and understand themselves well, their likes and dislikes, what they excel at, and what they find challenging; they gain lots of experience in analyzing situations and choosing which path forward to take; and their parents are close by to talk to while analyzing situations, available to share their experiences and thoughts. Young adults aren't left to ponder whether their choices are truly theirs, or are in reaction to their parents' control.

For parents, one of the significant advantages to allowing your children to make their own choices is that you are close by and easily available to provide whatever support and feedback your children might be looking for. Contrast that with dictating most of their childhood decisions until they move out on their own. This leaves them mostly alone to learn about themselves and figure out how they best function, just as they reach a point in their lives where the ramifications of their choices can be much greater.

But keep in mind that this is all at an appropriate level for the child. If she just wants you to grab an outfit out of her drawer and help her get dressed, do that; if she just wants some quick food to munch on while busily building with her Lego, just bring her a plate with some food that you're pretty sure she'll like; not all situations need analysis and defined choices. What's important is embracing the time and attention to discuss situations when the child sees options and is interested in choosing. Learning happens when there is interest.

In terms of learning and building their web of knowledge, choosing which threads to pursue now and which to leave for later also helps children build experience and confidence. Without choice in this area they aren't free to explore what they are most interested in, which is where the best learning is found. And if that thread they decided not to pursue last month comes up again this month related to something else, they begin to see that it might be a useful bit of information to have or skill to pick up and may soon choose to give it their attention.

> *As the parent, you can take a moment to look at the bigger picture and realize these are wonderful and exciting adventures to your child; more exciting to her than a clean living room would be to you.*

Notice a lot of these examples are not directly related to more academic learning. That should become less of a surprise as you ponder unschooling, or learning through living. A person doesn't typically think in terms of academic subjects outside of school. From the perspective of learning, these more academic topics and skills are intertwined in life, not separated out, as we discussed in Idea Two. When making choices, it's not, "Should I learn math or english today?" but maybe, "Do I want to work on programming that character interaction or write that game review this morning?" Remember, the best learning—learning that is understood and remembered—is in the living.

Let's look for a moment at those who grew up being taught to accept their parents' choices as best. Not only do they have minimal experience in analyzing situations, they have likely learned not to trust themselves. For example, if Samantha had had more experience with understanding herself and making choices, she may have realized that the law was really her father's dream, before applying to law school.

With big career-related choices, is a society-respected career (one many parents dream of for their children) right for everyone? Maybe being a trial lawyer is a great choice for Ellen, who loves to delve into conflicts in search of fine details and enjoys public speaking, but not for Samantha who went to law school because it was expected of her, even though she really excels at web design (her law firm now has a great website). Soon, Samantha is designing sites on the side for other clients, and eventually sets up her own design shop. Are Ellen's and Samantha's choices right or wrong? Neither, just different. But it may have been nice for Samantha if she'd realized this earlier and didn't drag herself through the years, and expense, of law school.

> *What's important is embracing the time and attention to discuss situations when the child sees options and is interested in choosing.*

Still, it's hard to classify Samantha's law school attendance as definitively wrong; it was more of a detour on her journey. As she got older she realized that being a lawyer was not interesting or fulfilling for her, but it was really just a different path, albeit a longer one, to the person she is today. But the sooner she discovers this about herself, the sooner her life is more enjoyable.

A person makes fewer detours as an adult if given the time and opportunities during childhood to really understand themselves, how they tick, and to incorporate that knowledge into their decision making when evaluating choices. Also, seeing how their perspective and goals change over time, especially during the teen years, helps them more easily understand and accept their changes of perspective and goals during adulthood, seeing them not as failures but as part of living. They are gaining real life experience.

Quitting Activities

Choosing to quit an activity is as much a learning experience as starting it. Think about that for a moment.

Six year-old Adam loves watching the Olympic swimmers in action and animatedly expresses an interest in doing that. You recommend swimming lessons. He thinks that sounds like fun so you register him for the next cycle of lessons at the local indoor pool. He excitedly gets dressed and packs up his bathing suit and towel on the day of his first lesson and joins his class on the pool deck, smiling at the teacher. Then he spends most of the class sitting at the edge of the pool as the teacher takes them one at a time into the water for a couple minutes, then back to the edge. He's disappointed at the end of the class, wishing he spent more time actually in the water. You talk with him about it, acknowledge his disenchantment, and mention that maybe the first week is more about getting organized and that next week he'll get more water time.

He is not quite as excited the next week as you gather his stuff and drive back to the pool. He joins his class on deck, but soon sees that

the second week is more of the same. When
you get home he says he doesn't want to go
back to that silly swimming class, it's not
fun.

This situation is not much fun for Adam and there isn't much learning about swimming going on either. In fact, if the environment for learning is negative it often casts a pall over the topic itself. If you insist that he continue attending he soon may actively begin to dislike swimming, even though it's mostly this particular lesson environment that he is unhappy with.

What is your goal here? To help Adam explore swimming? If so, and the swimming lessons aren't meeting that goal, then quitting seems to be a logical solution. Instead, you could try public swim times where you and he can play around in the water the whole time instead of sitting at the edge. Maybe consider private lessons where he'd spend the majority of his time in the water, not just short intervals. The point is, if your goal is to help your child explore an interest and that goal isn't being met, don't hesitate to move on. Not only does he continue learning about his interest (swimming), you both gain experience in finding the kind of learning environments that best fit him.

Or are you tempted to say that at this point your goal has become teaching Adam to fulfill his commitments? That he wanted to take this set of swimming lessons so he should finish them all and then he can decide not to take more? First, you risk turning him off swimming (or whatever the interest) altogether for the foreseeable future. Is that worth it?

And second, is it really a failure to quit something? Why? Is it a failure that your child discovers he isn't that interested in pursuing the activity after all? Or that this particular environment doesn't work well for him? Think about it. Is there really a good/ bad or success/failure judgment to be made when pursuing act-iveties? Isn't it more about exploring top-ics and environments to see which fit best individually? Are you worried your child won't take on challenges if not pressed? When the goal is truly important to them, children will doggedly pursue it, even through many challenging moments.

> *As a parent you don't need to teach this type of commitment by requiring it in everything they do; instead, help them find things that they enjoy so much that their dedication and learning flows naturally.*

Remember the determination when your child learned how to walk? That wasn't easy! Take a moment to think of something your child was, or is still, interested in. Pokemon? Skateboarding? Dancing? Dinosaurs? Remember how their face lit up as they dove into it? Their bubbling excitement when they talked about it? Even when they had a hard time beating the League Champion, or mastering their first skateboard ollie, or remembering that hip-hop dance combination, or were struggling to pronounce pachycephalosaur? Those were definitely challenging moments but their goal was important to them; they were so resolute and kept at it. As a parent you don't need to teach this type of commitment by requiring it in everything they do; instead, help them find things that they enjoy so much that their dedication and learning flows naturally. The key is exploring the world through their interests to discover what is truly important to them.

Children who have the freedom to explore a variety of things and discard them when they no longer make sense do not feel like failures when they choose to drop something. Instead they see it as another experience from which to learn a bit about something and a lot about themselves. This is a much better attitude than the child who is forced to stay, being told to suck it up and stick it out, who begins to feel powerless and resentful. As an adult this child is more likely, for example, to stay in an unhappy career so as not to look or feel like a failure, though he will definitely feel trapped.

Learning through experience, both how to analyze situations and choose the next step, and also how to courageously change paths when that choice doesn't work out as envisioned, is valuable; these are indispensable skills to bring into adulthood.

Philip Pullman illustrates this point wonderfully in The Amber Spyglass (2000).

> "What work have I got to do, then?" said Will, but went on at once, "No, on second thought, don't tell me. I shall decide what I do. If you say my work is fighting, or healing, or exploring, or whatever you might say, I'll always be thinking about it. And if I do end up doing that, I'll be resentful because it'll feel as if I didn't have a choice, and if I don't do it, I'll feel guilty because I should. Whatever I do, I will choose it, no one else."

> "Then you have already taken the first steps towards wisdom." said Zaphania.

It sums up human nature so succinctly, and describes what unschooling parents are trying to do: give their children the freedom to determine their own life's journey. And through each choice made and outcome lived, unschooled children gain experience with making choices, and in turn, learn more about the world and themselves.

IDEA FOUR: INSTEAD OF NO

Unschooling Paradigm ~ Why not yes?

Mainstream Paradigm: It is important for parents to set boundaries for their children, and a definitive no helps the parents stay in control.

Paradigm Shift: Saying *no* can make life seem easier in the moment, but saying *yes* encourages children to explore their world and cultivates their ability to live confidently in it.

The reflex, almost automatic, no accomplishes so much: it reminds the child where the power in the relationship sits; it discourages messes and inconvenience for the parent; and eventually it deters the child from bothering the parent in the first place. But what if those aren't your goals?

Analyzing Situations

Tammy is watching her favourite kid's show and they demonstrate how to make a paper bag puppet. She loves the idea and runs into the kitchen. "Mommy! Can we make a puppet? I saw how to do it on TV! We need a brown paper bag and the glue and some paper and some scissors and I'll get my crayons!" As you continue scrubbing the leftovers from the pot you answer, "No, I'm busy right now, Tammy." When she begs, "Please, Mom!" you reply, "When I'm done, honey." As usual, it takes longer than you expect and when you finally finish you notice it's getting late and start making dinner. After you all eat, now a couple hours after Tammy first asked, you offer to make a puppet with Tammy but she responds "No, thanks."

An automatic no to a child's request shuts down the path they were following, the connections they were making, and thus the learning that was happening in that moment. Typical parenting advice often touts the importance of maintaining boundaries for your child and the no answer seems to be the easiest way for most parents to feel like they've accomplished that, but at what cost? Being a gatekeeper to a child's activities keeps the relationship bound up in power. As the child gets older requests can become more about the power struggle than the activity itself and the relationship suffers.

Would you rather be a parent that supports their child's interests as much as possible? One who helps their child to explore the world? Do you prefer to see you and your child as a team working together? If so, then give your child's requests full consideration.

An automatic yes is just as thoughtless as a reflex no, but it is worth your time to ask yourself, "Why not?" Opening yourself up to the possibilities allows your child to explore what they find interesting, to learn more. And it gives you the opportunity to have some fun too—kids come up with some amazing ideas!

So take a breath and allow that automatic no to echo in your head for a beat. Then ask yourself, "Why not?" Critically examine the answers that pop into your head. "It's too messy." "It'll take too long." "I'm too busy." "It could be dangerous." Ask yourself follow-up questions to see if you're experiencing a knee-jerk reaction or whether the no holds up under examination. "Hmm. . . we could paint over a tarp in the basement." "We could start a game of Monopoly and leave it set up on the table to finish later." "He seems really excited to do this puzzle together; the dishes will still be there when we're done." "I could stand underneath as she plays on the monkey bars." As you begin seeing the possibilities beyond the no, mention them to your child and see if you can come up with a plan that *both* of you are happy with.

As it gets easier to move past the reflex no, you can move more directly into a conversation with your child about how to achieve what she's after—or just reply with a happy, "Yes!", and get to the fun. The more you are able to help your child accomplish and explore what piques her interest, the more your child will learn about herself and the world.

Rules versus Principles

Picking up the discarded wrapping paper from Bill's birthday gifts, you hear laughter coming from the living room. Curious, you poke your head around the corner just in time to see him tossing his new ball to his brother. "No throwing balls in the house!", you say sternly. They stop immediately and both look contrite as you turn to go. But noticing them both intently watching you as you leave the room, you decide it's best to take the ball with you, certain they were going to start up again as soon as you left.

Firm rules encourage knee-jerk no responses to children's questions and actions. Rules are often used as shortcuts—substitutes for thinking in the moment. Parents often fall back on them to avoid the need to evaluate each situation individually. And it can be tempting to pass these rules down to children as edicts rather than logical, thought-out conclusions. As a result, from a child's point of view, the rules often seem arbitrary. By relying on rules to respond to questions, you rob a child of the opportunity to analyze the situation and come to their own understanding and conclusion. You rob them of the opportunity to learn more about the world.

On the other hand, guiding principles allow you and your child to discuss situations together and to come up with unique solutions for each particular circumstance. Principles encourage discussion and evaluation of a situation, whereas rules shut discussion down. In my experience, parents learn interesting things as well in these discussions. We learn more about ourselves through sharing our thoughts and experiences. We learn more about our children and their interests, about what they are thinking, and what is motivating them. All great things!

Let's look at the situation above. What if you did not immediately jump to the rule? Instead you could pause, take a breath, and ask yourself, "Why not?" If in that moment you realize there is no real risk to them playing catch in the room, smile and take a moment to breathe in their fun—or better yet, join in the game! If you have concerns, share them, "Guys, there's some breakable stuff in here that I would like to keep safe." A principle. Now you have a starting point for conversation. "Can you go outside to play catch?" If they reply, "No, that won't work," keep going. You could ask them why. You might learn from their answers that right now Tom doesn't like playing active games when it's so hot outside, or that it's raining and you hadn't noticed. After a moment they may change their minds and want to play catch out in the rain! Or not. You could ask them if they have any ideas where they could play catch without risk of breaking things, or suggest another spot, "How about playing in the basement?" Or maybe they suggest moving the lamps to the corner, out of the way. If you think that'll work, you have a solution. If not, keep going.

What do the kids learn in these scenarios? In the rule-based *don't throw balls in the house* scenario, they are introduced to or reminded of the rule. The focus is on stopping them from playing catch. They don't learn the reasoning behind the rule. If they guess that it is so things won't get broken, they might conclude the rule is dumb—they can throw things around in the basement without breaking anything, so *not in the house* is just silly. But frustration because they have to stop playing likely deters them from even analyzing the situation at all. Next time they want to play catch in the house they'll remember the previous incident and be sure to check that there are no parents nearby.

In the principle-based *take care of our stuff* scenario, once someone is uncomfortable with what is happening, the children and parents analyze the situation together and work to find a solution. In this scenario, the focus is on helping them do what they want—to play catch. Everyone is working toward finding a way they can continue playing catch while taking care to minimize the risk of breaking things. They gain experience in analyzing a situation and considering the possibilities. Next time they want to play catch there's a good chance they'll remember the conversation and choose a spot accordingly.

See how the rule shuts down thinking and learning while the principle opens it up? Which one is more supportive of the parent-child relationship? Which parent would you rather be around?

Moving to Principles

Jade looks up, her eyes wide. "Really? No more rules?" You can see the intense concentration as she ponders the idea. "I can play on the computer as long as I want?" You smile and reply, "Yes!" She asks, "I can sleep in my favourite dress?" "Sure, if you want to," you agree. She turns and slowly wanders down the hall, shaking her head with a mixture of wonder and confusion.

As you begin seeing the advantage of living life as a family from the perspective of principles instead of rules it can be tempting to excitedly announce to your children that you have decided to toss the rules! Just as an automatic yes is as thoughtless as a knee-jerk no, chucking the rules out the window all at once for children used to them can create a free-for-all situation that doesn't support anyone. It can get downright miserable.

Imagine being Jade for a moment, a child who, until today, has been told to clean her plate before dessert, not throw balls in the house, go to bed at eight o'clock, and get dressed after breakfast. Imagine that you've been told these rules are for your own good because your parents love you and want the best for you. Even if you've been unhappy with the rules, what are you going to think if your parents suddenly declare that these rules no longer apply? Might you worry that they no longer care what you do? That they no longer want the best for you? No longer love you?

Or maybe you'll shout "Cool!" and think you have to take advantage of this opportunity before they change their minds. In your zeal, you eat ice cream for breakfast five days straight, stay up until two o'clock in the morning, play wildly and break some of your favourite toys, and finally collapse in a screaming mess on the living room floor before the end of the first week. This doesn't give you a chance to be yourself either.

How instead can you approach this paradigm shift from no to yes, from rules to principles so it doesn't turn your family life into chaos? Slowly and steadily over time, probably over a few months, situation by situation. Instead of watching the clock and announcing that it's time to go to bed, wait until they ask if they can stay up to watch the end of the movie, then you can answer "Sure, I'm enjoying it too, let's go to bed when it's over." Or think ahead and don't start the movie that night. "Let's watch the movie tomorrow because we need to wake up early in the morning to go to the zoo." Make it less about arbitrary rules and more about considering what you're all doing in the moment and beyond. Share

> *See how the rule shuts down thinking and learning while the principle opens it up? Which one is more supportive of the parent-child relationship? Which parent would you rather be around?*

your thoughts more so they begin to see how you think about and analyze situations.

As this analysis becomes the typical way of addressing questions you will all find you rely on rules less and less until they just aren't part of your family life any longer.

This paradigm shift begins to fundamentally change your concept of living together. You're no longer just related and living under the same roof, but growing together, living together as a team, helping and supporting each other, and respecting each other, regardless of age.

IDEA FIVE: LIVING TOGETHER

Unschooling Paradigm ~ Kids are people too.

Mainstream Paradigm: The parents' needs and wants are more important than the children's.

Paradigm Shift: It can seem that parents have, by virtue of age and childbirth, earned a position of power but everyone in the family has important needs and wants and can have a voice.

Children are often the second-class citizens of the family. Does giving them a voice in the family lead to chaos? How can we help them learn about themselves and how to live with others?

Learning to Live with Others

A loud crash spurs you downstairs in time to hear Max scream at his younger sister, "Why did you knock over my blocks?!" In between sobs Lisa says, "I want to play with them too!" Quickly sizing up the situation, you ask Max to share the blocks with his sister. "Mom, no! I need all the blocks for my tower!" As Lisa's cries grow louder, you try reasoning with him. "Max, you two played with the blocks together yesterday, please share some of the blocks with Lisa." Max groans in frustration, and losing patience, you issue an ultimatum, "Do what you're told or I'll put the blocks away so nobody can play with them!"

As you've worked to take a moment to check in with yourself when your child asks to do something, you've probably found there are often ways to support your child's exploration and learning by saying *yes*, even if you are initially thinking, "No way!"

Looking at situations analytically pushes the less relevant pieces of information to the back of your mind and you'll probably notice that the typical societal cries of *you're too young*, and *because I said so*, are some of the first defaults to erode. They are power-based responses that separate parents and children by virtue of age and family position without consideration for the actual situation at hand.

Instead, through conversations with your child, you begin seeing her as a person with ideas and feelings and goals, albeit with less life experience. Sometimes that works in her favour as she is keen to pursue her goals and will continue moving forward even when we, as parents with more experience, envision disappointment and caution against action. I have been surprised enough times by seeing things work out in the end to have learned to consider carefully whether to voice negative opinions.

In my experience, as I released the need for control over my children, they in turn picked up responsibility for themselves. As we began working together as a team and their trust in me grew, the need and struggle for power in our relationship faded away. We became collaborators, together figuring out ways to accomplish all of our goals.

If your family is currently living within a power-and-rules paradigm this can seem like a pipe dream, an invitation for wild behaviour and disaster to visit. Last chapter, I talked about moving slowly but resolutely toward dropping rules and focusing on principles. Discussion is a vital tool supporting principle-based living. As conflicts arise, drop the parental power paradigm and instead of reaching for a rule, start a conversation about the situation with those involved. Through these family discussions, you will begin building trust in your relationships with your children. They will build trust that you will listen to them and genuinely consider and incorporate their input. You will build trust that they are genuinely expressing their needs, not trying to take advantage of you. You will all gain confidence that the time spent to explore everyone's needs and discover a satisfying solution for everyone is time well spent.

In a power-and-rules paradigm, each family member is fighting for their share of the power. "I want to play with the blocks!" Even if the child doesn't really mind, they feel compelled to stake their boundaries, exert their power. Compromising with a sibling or parent can feel like an expression of weakness that may be used against them the next time. "You guys played with the blocks together yesterday."

It takes time to move through that outlook to a team-based one where the children—and parents—feel respected enough to release their need to feel powerful, trusting other family members to not take advantage of them. Relinquishing power is a slow process that is replaced by trust in each other. In this, the parents must lead by example. Show your children that you are willing to give all family members a voice in discussing current family issues and upcoming plans. Understand that at first your children may sense this as a display of weakness and try to take advantage of you by pushing for things that aren't overly important to them but that make them feel powerful within the family. They may suspect you will change your mind soon and re-exert your power through rules and may push to take advantage while they have the chance.

However, over time, as they see you taking their needs seriously and not struggling against them, see you are no longer fighting for power in the relationship, see you are sticking with this new way of parenting, they will begin feeling comfortable being themselves. They will slowly begin to relax, drop the posturing, and to bring to the discussion only the things that truly matter to them. They will no longer feel the need to demand five things in hopes of getting the two they really want. They will feel comfortable in just asking for those two, trusting, knowing, that you will do your best to help satisfy those two needs. Everyone begins feeling safe in being themselves, losing the need to project a tough exterior, to fight for their share of the power and consideration in the family.

The shift from manipulative, power-based relationships to a sincere, team-based approach where everyone feels heard and supported takes time but is incredibly satisfying for everyone involved. The sense of family that grows out of this process is extraordinary. These skills—listening to others' concerns, understanding and expressing our needs, analyzing alternatives, and narrowing in on a path forward that meets everyone's needs—are invaluable, and will be prized for life in all endeavours.

Learning about Themselves

"It's 8:30, time to go to bed!" Sally is downstairs pretending she didn't hear you. Nate has no such luck so he tries another tack, "Can I just watch the end of this show? Please?" "No, Nate. You stayed up last night. Tonight it's to bed on time." Trying yet another strategy he pronounces he's hungry, "Can I have a snack?" You sigh as you lean over the staircase to call to Sally. This happens every night.

We've seen that the freedom to pursue interests and make choices encourages our children to learn. Freedom works so well in the academic realm of learning that extending it into the realm of learning about living seems natural: learning about themselves, their personal eating and sleeping needs, and how they prefer their living environment arranged.

As you gain experience seeing the learning your children are doing every day, in every situation, your comfort level grows with the concept that the learning is in the living; the lines between living and learning blur, soon to be erased altogether. It's life.

> *It takes time to move through that outlook to a team-based one where the children— and parents—feel respected enough to release their need to feel powerful, trusting other family members to not take advantage of them.*

You've probably started considering some of these ideas on your own as you pondered the rules-versus-principles paradigm shift. You may have begun questioning bedtimes and mealtimes based on the clock instead of the people and events involved; sleeping arrangements based on current societal norms; food restrictions based on "good" and "bad" judgments; and set chores based solely on the parents' needs without the consideration of all family members.

Let's look at bedtimes. There are lots of great reasons for a person to get enough sleep, most notably health and mood. But who defines *enough*? And does it need to happen during a set time frame?

The person best able to define enough is the person doing the sleeping; regardless of when they go to sleep, they will sleep until they wake up. They are the best judge of how they feel: awake, tired, exhausted, sharp, cranky, or mellow. As a parent you can help them explore sleep and its relationship to mood and health by talking with them about it, about your experiences, what you observe, and helping them make their own personal connections.

When I mention talking with your child, I don't necessarily mean a targeted, sit-down, serious, *let's talk about sleep now* conversation where you explain in point form all the important reasons for sleep and ask your child to whip up their own sleeping schedule *right now please*. Instead, maybe a quick mention of the connection between illness recovery and sleeping as your child naps on the couch while fighting the flu; the brief acknowledgment of a comment as they make a connection between their feelings of frustration and level of tiredness. Do they want to sit down and talk about sleep in a more direct way? Go for it. Follow your child's lead. How do they want to learn more about it? Over the years they will experience staying up late, sleeping in, getting up early, being tired, sleeping soundly, sleeping fitfully—it's all part of life. And with all those situations they will learn how their body feels and gain experience in how their reactions serve them: Did a nap help? Going earlier to bed? Do they need a few days to shift their sleeping patterns? Do they feel best after seven, eight, nine hours of sleep?

In addition, you can talk about upcoming plans so they are working with the full picture as they choose when to go to bed. Do you plan on getting up early tomorrow to go to the Science Centre or to visit friends? Figure out together what time you want to leave in the morning and suggest they may want to get to bed by such-and-such a time for a full night's sleep-based on whatever they feel a *full night* is for them. And if they don't follow your suggestion, don't fret. Maybe you'll learn that your child can wake up and enjoy an exciting day out after less sleep than usual; maybe your child will learn that they doesn't have as much fun when they're out and about but tired. Or maybe you'll all decide to postpone the trip to another day. Or, if it's a firm commitment, maybe you can help them get to sleep more easily with a familiar movie, in a darkened room, cuddled in a blanket. So many choices. In any given situation the learning may not be what you first expect, but there is useful learning nonetheless. And remember, it may take a number of repeat experiences until your child draws certain conclusions and incorporates them into their decision making; it is human nature to retest a hypothesis.

The lack of an arbitrary bedtime does not mean the absence of a bedtime routine if that's something your child enjoys. Many children, especially younger ones, find a bedtime routine helpful in settling down for sleep—a bath, fresh pyjamas, a story or three. If you notice they are getting tired and are amenable, start the routine to wind down. Other children prefer going until they drop, or hanging out quietly with their parents until they drift off to sleep. Understanding how they prefer getting to sleep is a useful, lifelong skill—and it may look nothing like how you prefer to welcome slumber.

So far we've discussed the *when* of sleeping; how about the *where*? What do you think of the societal expectation that children sleep in their own bed, in their own room from a very early age? What are your goals regarding sleep and your family? That everyone get the best quality sleep? Is that more important than where they happen to be when they get it? If your child sleeps better with you near, a family bed might be a great solution. Or maybe more of a sleeping room configuration, with a mattress on the floor in your room so you are still nearby. A child that feels loved and supported, and has had a good night's sleep, is in a much better frame of mind for pursuing all the living and learning that the new day will bring!

Let's move from sleep to food. The same concepts regarding bedtimes also apply to mealtimes; it is better for our health to respond to our unique body's needs rather than to be led by a clock. Eat when your body is hungry, not when it is eight or twelve or six o'clock. Allow your child, and yourself, the space to listen to what your body is telling you.

Everything above about bedtimes applies to mealtimes as well:

- the best person to define hungry or full is the person doing the eating;

- mealtime routines may be enjoyed by some;

- the experiences of eating too much, too little, being hungry, feeling nauseated, noticing food that makes them feel good, or food that they react negatively to, and more, will give them information to figure out how they and food work together.

It's all part of life and learning. The principle of listening to your body's needs applies logically to both sleeping and eating. Now let's delve deeper into another aspect of food: *what* they eat.

Food advice is shouted almost fanatically from many corners: health organizations, food producers, children's groups, food sellers. And most of it is trying to convince you to control food rigorously. There's good food, bad food, junk food, fat-free food, low carb food, comfort food. Food nicknames evoke an emotional response in an effort to control your food dollar. You feel like a *good* parent when you say no to your child's request for a bag of chips or another pop, and instead give your child a good snack of carrots and yogurt dip. But are you really helping your child develop healthy eating habits by restricting their access to things you deem unacceptable? Have you thought it through yourself or are you accepting the messages that are flying around? Do you follow the same eating habits you impose on your children? Is it a challenge? It can be difficult because you are setting yourself, and your child, up against human nature.

It is human nature to want what is restricted. Think about it. For lunch you are sitting in front of a nice big salad and you can eat as much of it as you want. On a side dish you also have two of your favourite cookies to enjoy, but no more. What do your thoughts revolve around as you sit down to eat? Most likely the cookies. Should I eat them first? Last? Interspersed with the salad? Why do they live at the forefront of your mind during your meal? Because they are restricted, and as such, gain a special status. You only get two so you have to think and plan around them to get the most satisfaction possible from those two cookies. Why think of the salad when you can have as much of that as you like, no thinking required?

When my children were younger, I did restrict their access to sugary treats as recommended by so many parenting books and articles. (Doesn't the nickname make them seem even more appealing?) Inevitably, when there was a box of cookies or chocolate around it seemed an almost unending round of requests and refusals. No wonder parents imagine that without restrictions that's all their children would eat! But I found, as other unschooling parents I know have before me, once the artificial restriction is lifted and access is free, that it becomes just one of many choices. This allows other factors to come into play: Am I hungry? Do I actually fancy something sweet? Will some protein hit the spot better? These are much more useful questions to ask yourself, rather than just trying to eat as much of something as you can get away with.

Don't be surprised though, if they binge at first with the joy of access to previously restricted food. Again, they'll likely want to take advantage of the opportunity, unsure how long it will last. Once that fear diminishes, forbidden fruits lose their lofty status and children are free to listen to their body's needs instead. Back to the principle of learning and following your body's unique needs.

There is a third aspect to eating—where. As a family, how important is this aspect? Must all food be eaten at the kitchen table? Why? Is your child busily engaged with their passion, yet also hungry? Do they ask if they can eat their sandwich while they continue their activity? Check in with yourself. What's your goal? To get their basic physiological need for food met? That can be met anywhere as long as they are eating. Do you really want to interrupt the flow of their playing and learning by expecting them to stop what they are doing and come to the table to eat? In that situation they may choose not to eat but to continue their activity instead, going without and wearing down their body, maybe slowing down their learning as their concentration fades with growing hunger and frustration.

If one of your important goals is to support their learning, bringing food and drink to them in situations where they are fully engaged and eager to continue can be a great solution. If this seems like a hardship, take a moment to examine why. You're still making the food, just taking it a few steps further to another room. If you are concerned about leaving dirty dishes around, mention that. How about when your child next takes a break, go grab the dishes and ask for help to bring them back to the kitchen. If you're concerned about crumbs making a mess, have a brief conversation about that. Maybe you and your child will decide to eat a less crumbly snack, or to place a towel on their lap for easier cleanup. There are always many options on the spectrum between yes and no if those involved take a moment to brainstorm the possibilities. The idea is to match what truly needs to be done within the flow of the day's activities—not the other way around.

This leads into another parenting area—chores. Again, what is your goal? If you as a parent decide what housework needs to be done and divvy it up between you and your children, what are they learning? They are working to meet your needs with respect to the home environment, not discovering their own. Often a child brought up with chores will enthusiastically not do any house cleaning when first on their own—they need to get far away from the expectation before they can begin discovering what their own needs are in that area. Almost like rebounding from food restrictions, they are binging on the freedom of not having to tidy and clean.

Instead, with the freedom to wait until they see a need to tidy or clean, and the freedom to say yes or no when asked to help out with a certain task around the house, children can discover their own preferences for their environment. Does their room look messy to outsiders but your child knows exactly where everything is? Do they like to have everything in its place? Do they not mind the mess for a while, but are excited at the clean slate they see after you've tidied up? Through these experiences they will learn how they like their surroundings, and as they grow up they will likely help out to maintain it that way. I know as my children have gotten older they will tend to their rooms as they best enjoy them. My eldest son likes everything in its place and no messy area will last more than a few hours; my daughter doesn't mind the messy look but when she's had enough she will happily ensconce herself in her room for the day to tidy up; my youngest son falls somewhere in between.

However, general housework is the one area in which my children have received mixed messages and it shows.

Their Dad will, from time to time, speak to them about expecting them to help out more around the house. The challenge with this is that it is often voiced as a generalized expectation. Because of this, as I have discovered in conversation with them, they are reluctant to help for a while after the request, even if they normally would, feeling that the expectation has created a situation where helping out will be seen as an implicit agreement to continue helping out, that it might be interpreted by their Dad as an act of admission that they have not been *helping out enough*. Here, helping out actually morphs from being a positive experience to an inadvertent admission of failure. Who wants to do that?

That's the danger of expectations; they often backfire because the normal human response is to avoid fulfilling them completely. Think about a time when expectations were placed on you. How did you respond? I wonder how you would feel if your spouse said to you, "I expect you to vacuum the house every week," or "I expect you to have the dishes cleaned before you read your book." Even if you felt that a once-a-week vacuum was reasonable, and you preferred to finish up the dishes and tidy the kitchen before settling into your book, it's likely you would loath doing so now that someone is expecting it of you. Why? Because you are no longer choosing to do the task of your own volition; the sense of accomplishment has been taken away from you because now what you're accomplishing is the completion of your spouse's demand, not the task at hand. There's a yucky layer of expectation over the task that has marred the whole experience by taking the control out of your hands and giving it to another.

Tying chores to allowances does essentially the same thing—sets up expectations by tying regular home tasks to rewards. On one hand it sets up an unrealistic situation; when they move out on their own they won't get paid for keeping their own house. On the other hand, I *want* them to have some of their own money, *not to be continually withholding it as punishment*. That sets up a layer of antagonism in our relationship with little gain. Again, with learning as my goal, I want them to have some money to explore and learn with! How does it feel to make that impulse buy? How satisfying is it to save up for that bigger purchase? What is the deal with quality versus price? Does it typically hold? Ah, marketing. When that advertisement convinces him to buy that high-priced toy, does he really get more satisfaction from it? Does name brand make a difference? Sure I share my thoughts, but to really learn they need to explore the consumer world, to be hands-on. And better to do that growing up when the toys are much less expensive, (versus adult toys like big screen TVs, cars, and fancy purses) and I'm around to discuss it all with them.

Moving On Out

At your spouse's work picnic the conversation drifts to kids. Ray, one of the dads you just met, complains loudly, "My kid is sixteen and is so cranky! He won't get a job and he won't help around the house. When he turns eighteen, either he moves out or he starts paying rent! Then he'll know what the real world is like." Many of the other parents

gathered   around   nod   their   head   in

understanding and agreement.

Preparing my kids for eventually moving out their own is an important goal I see for myself as a parent. But the goal is not that my children move out as soon as possible. It is to have supported and helped them gain the knowledge and skills that will help make the transition to living on their own as trouble free as possible. I have come to realize that unschooling isn't exclusively about school, or the replacement of school. Working toward graduation is too short-sighted because it only lasts twelve or so years of their life, at least the compulsory version. Unschooling is about *life*, about helping children grow as human beings from birth to adulthood. Growing up in an unschooling family, children are already experienced at making everyday choices, from what, when, and where to eat to when, where, and how long to sleep. They will understand themselves and their needs and be able to communicate them to their friends, to their work colleagues, to their parents. And they'll have some experience living with their changing needs too. They will have lots of experience in learning on their own, understanding how they best learn new things, and will continue learning with joy and excitement, whether it's a personal interest or hobby, or a new work-related skill.

Before it seems too good to be true, realize that unschooling doesn't protect anyone from life's challenges. Maybe your child is wishing for more friends, or feeling sad, or facing physical or emotional challenges; these aren't the exclusive domain of school kids, they are part of life, of living. But unschooling through these more difficult times has advantages. School demands and issues aren't piled on top of it all as well, and you are with your child to help them work through it as much as they need and want, at any age.

Unschooled young adults are comfortable enough with themselves to choose when *they* are ready to move out into the adult world—not when the parent thinks they should move out, not as soon as it is legally possible to escape an overbearing home environment, but when they feel ready to take that next step. Years of respectfully being given the time and support to explore and learn in the world, to apply their growing life skills again and again in pursuit of experience and knowledge, to work through the challenges that life scatters in their path helps them more successfully transition to life on their own. Or discover they aren't quite ready and come back home for a while without shame. They know they have their parents support as they navigate life.

Children need the space and support to discover how they evolve with age and life experience. If they don't get the time to understand themselves and discover their dreams and passions growing up, they may need to take it as young adults, going off to find themselves. If they miss it then, they may just continue pursuing what they have been told will bring them happiness: the good job, the right car, the perfect family and so on.

Maybe they will manage to hang on for a couple more decades, though they may wear, as Dean Sluyter in *Cinema Nirvana* (2005, 70) puts it, "the drained, dispirited faces of silent adults—postop cases who have already undergone the freedomectomy." Then the midlife crisis hits. "Is this really what I want to do with my life?" "Am I really happy?" Divorces, drastic career changes are all part and parcel of waiting until midlife to take the time to really know and understand yourself, what makes you tick, what brings you joy.

The unschooling lifestyle—one where everyone in the family is considered a full team member, regardless of age; where everyone is given space and respect to explore their personal needs for sleep, food, enjoyment, and their living environment; where everyone is free to learn—gives each child a wonderful combination of knowledge, skills, and experience to move out into the world as an adult.

PUTTING IT ALL TOGETHER

When I first came to unschooling, I concentrated on the concept of learning. That's what the school system was providing, right? So initially my focus was on how my children would learn at home versus how they were learning at school. What I found was that when I looked at real learning, learning that was understood and remembered, the potential for it was much greater when living directly in the real world versus spending a large part of the day in a classroom learning from a simulated world.

In *Free to Learn* I have concentrated on sharing ways to support our children's real learning:

> - by looking at learning through the learner's eyes instead of a teacher's;

- by understanding that learning happens most successfully when the learner is interested and engaged;

- by realizing that learning *how* to make choices, rather than being told what choices to make, is a very useful life skill;

- by stopping to think as situations arise and discussing possible options together, rather than leaning on rules; and

- by understanding that everyone in the family has important needs and can have a voice without chaos ensuing.

However, a couple interesting things happened along the way. As I was making these paradigm shifts I uncovered an underlying theme: trust. While living and learning together, I sometimes didn't understand my children's needs or wishes. Why was it so important to him to stay home yet again? Why did she not want to come play with the paints? It was during those moments that I most needed to remember the above points and trust that learning was still happening, even if I didn't grasp it in the moment. Just because I didn't understand the situation did not mean that it didn't have the same value for my child as a situation that was more transparent to me. So though I have focused on learning, I have also mentioned developing trust in various places. Having a high level of trust in your children does *not* mean that you leave them alone more. You are still living together, bringing fun and interesting things and ideas into each other's lives, chatting, discussing, and sharing. This level of trust and understanding of your kids and their lives will lessen your fear for your kids in general. And with this trust comes true respect, a deep sense of the inherent worth of your children, which I have found to be reciprocated in abundance.

> *Remember to make these changes with the intention to move forward, not just to drop the mainstream paradigms. The shift to new paradigms is crucial or your children may feel abandoned and unsupported, and alone in navigating life.*

Once I had worked my way through these paradigm shifts, I understood that real learning was happening all the time and I trusted their learning and choices, even when I didn't clearly see the connections myself. Through that deep trust in my children, I saw that they were living full and joyful lives and soon came to the realization that focusing my parenting on completing my "job" while they are school aged was very limiting. We are a family, and we'll continue to live and learn together throughout our lives, still connected even if we don't live under the same roof. And with no graduation date looming where they would celebrate having finished learning, I know their love of learning will not fade over time. Eventually, watching for learning dropped off my radar and the true focus began to emerge—our relationships.

Looking at unschooling through a relationship lens, it becomes quite clear that the paradigm shifts I underwent were also those that most improved our relationships. Try rereading Free to Learn with an eye to your family relationships and regularly ask yourself, "Would this help or hinder my relationship with my child?"

Also, I would like to repeat what I mentioned in the introduction. Don't just skim through the ideas, logical as they may seem on the surface. Really live with them. Let them ruminate in the back of your mind as you go about your day. Recall your own learning experiences, in school and out, and see how they compare. It will take work on your part to deeply understand these concepts and bring them into the everyday life of your family, but it will be truly rewarding.

Hold these ideas, these unschooling principles, in your mind throughout the day and examine them in light of your family. Observe how things happen now, and consider how they may unfold if your actions were grounded in these ideas. As you dig deeper into the ideas I've been talking about, you will likely find yourself making choices that align more with your developing appreciation of real learning and living together. Remember to make these changes with the intention to move forward, not just to drop the mainstream paradigms. The *shift* to new paradigms is crucial or your children may feel abandoned and unsupported, and alone in navigating life.

I think you'll find that not only do these five ideas create an optimal learning environment for your children, living them also best supports the development of loving and respectful relationships with your children. And these amazing relationships will last a lifetime.

REFERENCES

Canadian Oxford Dictionary, 2nd ed., s.v. "paradigm shift."

Canadian Oxford Dictionary, 2nd ed., s.v. "paradigm."

Holt, John. 1983. *How Children Learn*. New York: Dell.

Irwin, William, Mark T. Conrad, and Aeon J. Skoble, eds. 2001. *The Simpsons and Philosophy: The D'Oh of Homer*. Popular Culture and Philosophy, vol. 2. Chicago: Open Court Publishing.

Poe, Edgar Allen. 2003. *The Raven and Other Writings*. New York: Simon & Schuster.

Pullman, Philip. 2000. *The Amber Spyglass*. New York: Random House.

Reduced Shakespeare Company, The. *The Complete Works of WilliamShakespeare (abridged)*. DVD. Directed by Paul Kafno. 2000.

Simpsons, The. "Tales from the Public Domain". Season 13, episode 14. Written by Andrew Kreisberg, Josh Lieb, and Matt Warburton. Directed by Mike B. Anderson. Originally aired March 17, 2002, Fox network. Released August 24, 2010 as part of *The Simpsons: The Complete Thirteenth Season*. DVD

Simpsons, The. "Treehouse of Horror". Season 2, episode 3. Written by Sam Simon and Edgar Allen Poe. Directed by David Silverman. Originally aired October 25, 1990, Fox network.

Sluyter, Dean. 2005. *Cinema Nirvana: Enlightenment Lessons from the Movies*. New York: Random House.

Toffler, Alvin. 1998. *Future Shock*. New York: Random House.

ADDITIONAL READING

This is by no means an exhaustive list but it will help you get your feet wet!

Parenting a Free Child: An Unschooled Life
by Rue Kream

This terrific book is written in question and answer format, with both unschooling-specific and parenting questions. As one of the reviewers wrote: "Rue addresses clearly and persuasively the most common questions and objections in an easily accessible format. The personal experience and conviction brought to each answer shines through along with her deep love and respect for her children." So true!

Big Book of Unschooling
by Sandra Dodd

Would you like to have a printed and bound version of Sandra's huge website? Here it is! She's hand-picked many of the thoughts and insights found on her website and brought them together here.

Moving a Puddle and other essays
by Sandra Dodd

Sandra has pulled together forty-eight of her essays and published them in easy-to-read book format. The overall theme is how learning, parenting and everyday life can be in the absence of school, viewed from different vantage points over a dozen years.

The Teenage Liberation Handbook: How to Quit School and Get a Real Life and Education
by Grace Llewellyn

An "unschooling handbook" for older kids, it has almost reached cult status!

The Willed Curriculum, Unschooling, and Self-Direction
by Carlo Ricci

Carlo spoke at my unschooling conference, TUC, three of its six years. He is a staunch defender of children's rights and founder of JUAL, the online Journal of Unschooling and Alternative Learning.

Teach Your Own
by John Holt

In fact, anything by John Holt: *Learning All The Time, How Children Fail, How Children Learn* and others. Considered the "father" of unschooling by many (though he never had children of his own), his books recount his journey from school teacher to unschooling advocate.

The Unprocessed Child: Living Without School
by Valerie Fitzenreiter

A wonderful book about raising a child in an unschooling lifestyle. It's great to read about unschooling in action, not just in theory.

The Unschooling Handbook: How to Use the Whole World As Your Child's Classroom
by Mary Griffith

This book is a really great introduction to the world of unschooling. She gives an overview of unschooling, takes a look at the kinds of materials we learn from, discusses documentation, gives examples of the unschooling approach to learning in some basic subject areas, and looks at some of the other issues involved with unschooling. The book is full of anecdotes from other unschooling parents, and some from unschooling kids themselves.

The Homeschooling Book of Answers: The 88 Most Important Questions Answered by Homeschooling's Most Respected Voices
by Linda Dobson

Not specifically an unschooling book, but it is quite unschooly. It's a good book for answers to all those nagging little questions, in your mind as well as in the minds of well-meaning relatives and friends!

Family Matters: Why Homeschooling Makes Sense
by David Guterson

He gives an interesting perspective as high school teacher and a homeschooling parent.

Dumbing Us Down: The Hidden Curriculum of Compulsory Schooling
by John Taylor Gatto

Though not an unschooling book at all, it's collection of essays from a long time public school teacher that clearly describe many of the problems with formal schooling. His acceptance speech for New York Teacher of the Year in 1991 is very compelling: "The Seven-Lesson Schoolteacher."

LifeLearningMagazine.com

A great online magazine about self-directed learning. It's a family-run business that has been supporting life learning, or unschooling, for many years.

LivingJoyfully.ca

This is my website, where you'll find even more information about unschooling, and my blog.

SandraDodd.com/unschooling

Sandra has written a lot of wonderful things about unschooling over the years. She has also collected many pearls of wisdom from other unschoolers that participate with her on various emails lists and message boards and has woven them throughout her website.

JoyfullyRejoycing.com

Joyce Fetteroll has pulled together a terrific site full of her replies over the years on all the most popular unschooling topics—it is overflowing of amazing tidbits and insights. She has such a clear and concise way with words!

BestHomeschooling.org

Lillian Jones asks some experienced homeschoolers "What's your best homeschooling advice?" She has a great selection of articles plus more links to follow.

NaturalChild.org

The Natural Child Project is Jan Hunt's wonderful website. Go to the articles section and click on Learning to get to some great reading! Be sure to check out "What is Unschooling?" by Earl Stevens if you're just getting started. And if you have time, check out the rest of the site too—it's terrific!

fraserinstitute.org/research-news/
display.aspx?id=13089

is a direct link to "Homeschooling: From the Extreme to the mainstream, 2nd edition" research paper by the Fraser Institute (an independent public policy organization in Canada) first published in 2001 that was so popular they published a second edition in 2007. Here's an excerpt from the executive summary:

Many studies, Canadian, American, and international, have found that home schooled students outperform students in both public and independent (private) schools. One US study found that home and private school students perform comparably well, and that both maintain a strong advantage over public school students.

You can download the pdf version free at the link.

18740930R00065

Made in the USA
Charleston, SC
18 April 2013